CAN GRANDPA PLAY RACQUETBALL?

Published by
Jubilant Enterprises, Inc.

78 79 80 81   10 9 8 7 6 5 4 3 2

Dedicated to
my wife, Shirley
and family

This book could not have been written without the encouragement they have given me
in racquetball and all that I do.

Also, to
my racquetball buddies who encouraged me
to write the book, to Ruth Palmer for typ-
ing drafts of original text, and to Adelle
Barnett for editorial suggestions.

Plus
a further debt of gratitude is due to my
daughter, Linda H. Bennett for illustrating
concepts discussed in the book.

FOREWORD

Many American senior citizens today are not doing the things that are good for them.

It is my belief that as a person ages he becomes less active, and as a consequence his physical body, as well as his mind deteriorates. The recommended antidote for this is activity. Further, an alternative which produces physical benefits while being enjoyable is racquetball.

I would like to think that some people reading a book on this sport would decide that they would like to try the game. By taking up racquetball, those people may be helped by a game that will be both socially enjoyable and physically beneficial to them.

—W. E. Hight

TABLE OF CONTENTS

Can Grandpa Play Racquetball?

Okay, Grandpa. If you haven't already been asked to play some game with your grandchildren, the day is surely coming when you shall have the question put to you. Are you ready to answer the invitation? Or, if you have already given a negative answer, do you believe your response was a fair one?

You know, the time arrives with most of us when our hearts turn toward our children and their children; and hopefully their hearts may be turned toward us. Whether we then have their interest may well be the result of companionship we share with them in their younger years.

Indeed, playing with the younger folk is one of the better ways to become their trusted companions. I think of Judge Allan Crockett who has had occasion to note many personal tragedies from the bench. Most every Saturday he can be seen spending time with his granddaughters at the Deseret Gym in Salt Lake City. A wise man —Judge Crockett.

So, what will your answer be? But, you say, you're not in shape—it's been years since you've been physically active. You'd better get a medical examination and re-assess what physical condition you are really in.

Can Grandpa play racquetball?

What is Grandpa Doing?

There are two kinds of grandpas, physically speaking. There are the inactive grandpas who have limited interests, and there are the active grandpas.

Contributing to inactivity is a tendency in later adulthood to become addicted to TV watching. The consequence of this is that there is a lessening of the activity that keeps up the physical body. There is an inclination to look for chair comfort to accommodate a considerable amount of sitting.

I remember my own father who strictly limited his activity in later life. I think of my dad's long sittings at the kitchen table, reading a book and drinking a beverage. Such inclination of senior citizens to occupy themselves in sedentary activities—playing solitaire, watching TV, etc., results in a loss of muscle tone in the body, and even an atrophy of the body muscles as they wither from lack of use.

Is time hanging heavy with Grandpa?

Contrasted to this category of inactive senior citizens are the healthy grandpas in the active category. Among the active grandpas, I think of Frank Nebeker, who at the age of sixty retired from work, and the following week appeared at the gym and began to learn the game of racquetball. One of his companions and regular racquetball buddies, Stan Russon, is seventy-two. His interests include the dramatic arts, playing supporting lead roles in musical productions, and regularly exercising at the Deseret Gym in Salt Lake City by beginning his day playing racquetball.

Let me introduce you to Luzell Wilde, through the following excerpts from an article in the 2 March 1978 issue of the Salt Lake Tribune:

Roomfull of Trophies
At Age 60,
He Masters Racquetball Sport
By Walt Schaffer
Tribune Staff Writer

Luzell D. Wilde started playing racquetball about 10 years ago when the sport was just getting off the ground in Utah. Since that time, he has amassed a roomfull of trophies and competes with the best in the sport, at age 60.

"I was never really active in a particular sport until racquetball," said Mr. Wilde. "Now I practice about four days a week and enjoy the competition."

Mr. Wilde's game needs little improvement as demonstrated by his last weekend win in the masters' bracket of the Utah State Racquetball Championships at the Deseret Gymnasium.

In April 1977, Mr. Wilde finished third in the Western Regionals in Reno; and June of the same year, he captured fourth place in nationals singles and third place in doubles at the Pro-Am national racquetball matches in San Diego, Calif. In February 1978, he garnered second place in singles in the Colgate Men & Women's Pro-Am Southwest Regionals, Tempe, Ariz.

With a desk strewn with racquetball magazine tournament applications, rule books and handbooks, Mr. Wilde keeps abreast of changes in the sport while at the same time eager to talk about his game, or better yet, meet you on the court.

For further examples of active grandpas, consider the lives of five senior men as reported 9 July 1973; reprinted by permission of the Salt Lake Tribune as follows:

GYM REPLACES ROCKING CHAIR
by Steve Wilson
Tribune Sports Writer

Those grand old souls 65 years of age and older have been called everything from the "rocking chair set" to the "warm milk and aspirin for lunch bunch."

And it's really not surprising. There's a sad tendency among members of the retirement age clan to comfort themselves with "Well, I've lived a good life." And settle back for what remains of a dreary existence.

Enter five stout-hearted men who shoot this stereo-type all to pieces.

Milton Backman, D. Clyde "Mouse" Lloyd, Eli Lecheminant, Ray Sorensen, and Judge Allan Crockett are athletes, darned good ones at that.

This quintet gathers frequently at the Deseret Gym for a few games of racquetball, the variation of handball you play with a paddle.

The only thing is, four of these gentlemen are over 70 years old and the other, the "baby" of the group is 67.

"I feel as young as I did when I was 30," said Backman, a soft-spoken man of 74 who, despite his increasing years, still practices law in Salt Lake City.

Proving age has no bearing on physical activity, Milton Backman, D. Clyde "Mouse" Lloyd, Judge Allan Crockett, Ray Sorensen and Eli Lecheminant, left to right, get ready for racquetball contest.

Five "seniors" playing racquetball.

Reputed to be one of the most active around, Backman rests only on Sunday. "I play racquetball here at the Gym on Mondays, Wednesdays and Fridays and reserve Tuesdays, Thursdays and Saturdays for golf," he noted with some pride.

"Mouse" Lloyd, a wiry little man who lists his age as 72, played the part of a rodent in a first-grade play. Thus the nickname.

Aside from sports, which have occupied much of his life, "Mouse" found time to become an author.

"I've published three books of poetry," he said proudly. "All my stuff is philosophical, not any of this Roses are Red business."

"Mouse" is still a solid singles player, as his racquetball opponents quickly point out.

Eli Lecheminant, also 72, but with the physique and countenance of a man much younger, likes the association he receives from racquetball.

"I'm gregarious," he said. "That's enough to keep me going."

Now to the two extremes of this little group, oldest and youngest.

"I'm just old on the inside," joked 76-

year-old Ray Sorensen, the most elderly member of this supposedly "over-the-hill" gang.

And judging from the way he bounced around striking athletic poses and chattering like a distraught magpie, you had to believe him.

Sorensen, a former speed skating champion, has been a Deseret Gym member since 1915.

Judge Allan Crockett, a fixture in Salt Lake City courtrooms, is equally conspicuous on the racquetball court because, as an observer stressed, "he gives any player a tough game in doubles and is one of the very finest players we have at the Gym."

At 67, Judge Crockett is the youngster, the only one in this collection of five not over 70.

"My job, as one might suspect, is sedentary," the judge explained. "I'm sitting down all the time and I need the exercise racquetball gives me. If I didn't spend the noon hour at the Gym I'd go stir crazy."

So, there's no need to become permanently depressed when you reach the age of 65. If all senior citizens had the youthful vigor of these five ageless athletes, the rest homes would go out of business."

Look at these five men in 1978

Lloyd – Backman – Crockett

The life styles of "Mouse" Lloyd, Milt Backman, and Judge Crockett are increasingly amazing, being basically unchanged though they are five years older, now averaging 76 years old. Despite the increased age, they are still winning racquetball games.

LeCheminant   *Sorensen*

Ray Sorensen, at this time spends much of his day taking care of an elderly person in failing health. However, he appears to be decades younger than his own actual age of 81.

Eli LeCheminant gives full time in charitable work, typically beginning his day before 5 AM. In the afternoon of a typical day he now plays nine holes of golf, and in the evening takes his wife out dining. All this at age 77.

Today (1978) this active group now averages 77 years of age and they're still going strong. In summary, let us review what our grandpas are doing. Has grandpa limited his physical activity, or has he continued physical exercises, enjoying good health and friendly associations? This brings us to the question: "Why should grandpa play racquetball?"

Why Should Grandpa Play Racquetball?

Consider some observations based upon a news editor's discussions with Elder Marion D. Hanks, a general authority of The Church of Jesus Christ of Latter-day Saints, long identified with the Church's youth program, and who is a member of the President's Council on Physical Fitness and Sports.

"We have a very questionable state of healthy—nationally. We know that at least 49 million Americans, by survey, do nothing in terms of any specific effort to exercise and take care of themselves physically. It is this group that needs to be reached," Elder Hanks said.

Recognizing that physical fitness is an essential quality for any one desiring to make the most of himself and his life, Elder Hanks outlined the goals of the President's council as a society in which regular exercise, participation in sports and games and good health care are an established way of life for both young and old alike.

For adults, one hour of vigorous physical activity each day, through work or play, will improve appearance, performance and may prolong life, according to the published goals of the council.

Most medical authorities join active people in the belief that exercise helps a person feel, look and work better.

(The above excerpts, printed by permission, were from an article written by J. M. Heslop in the 13 July 1974 issue of the Deseret News).

I believe that racquetball is a sport which qualifies as an activity conducive to good health. Further, it may reduce our susceptibility to two prevalent afflictions among oldsters; namely, obesity and "spectatoritis," watching physical activities rather than participating in them.

In playing racquetball, participants may burn sufficient calories to avoid gaining weight, and certainly "spectatoritis" is not a part of that life style.

Also, playing racquetball is one of the exercises that can be enjoyed while maintaining healthy heart and lungs. The good health of these primary organs may well slow up the deterioration of the rest of the body.

On the other hand, if daily activity fails to properly exercise the heart and lungs, then you are in trouble.

Consider my personal experience.

After more than a decade of confining work in accounting, I found it necessary, in my mid-forties, to be hospitalized because of a collapsed right lung. I remember the circumstances preceding the hospitalization. I was riding the bus to and from work at the time. To meet work deadlines, I carried heavy brief cases with me on the bus. In the exercise of poor judgment I usually rode the last bus home, but would often leave the office so late, I had to run two or three blocks to the bus stop, carrying the heavy brief case. My problem was that my memory was far superior to my judgment, for I could remember earlier years when I could run a mile or more at a stretch without noticing problems.

It took my doctor to explain to me that an aging process was taking place. The elasticity which my lungs earlier possessed had given way to brittleness, and a part of the lung had snapped like an old rubber band. In the recuperative period following the surgical procedure to re-inflate my lung, my doctor suggested that I take walks, and later jog as a regular exercise to retard the aging process.

Some months later upon a re-examination, my doctor asked if I were jogging. I said, "No, but I am playing racquetball."

How am I, Doc? Can I play racquetball?

Doc said: "Well, I have no quarrel with that in your case. I suggest you keep on regularly doing what you're doing."

Now, I don't pretend to have the medical judgment to know what exercises you grandpas should be doing; but with the assurance of my doctor that racquetball, played regularly and sensibly, is a good physical activity for me, I am getting the fullest value of an annual gymnasium membership, by greatly enjoying the fast-growing popular sport of racquetball. I therefore suggest that you counsel with your doctor to see if this sport would not also be enjoyable and physically beneficial to you.

The enjoyment of the game is part of the benefit. Racquetball is easy to learn. Within an hour of playing in the racquetball court, you can find that you are able to play reasonably well, and the enjoyment you find will allow you to develop further proficiency in the sport.

Some of the favorable aspects I see in racquetball are the following:

It is easy to get into a game of racquetball. Consider, for example, that you may have been a football player in high school and you may well have enjoyed the sport. What happens, however, after all your teammates graduate from school and you decide that you would like to enjoy the game you once played? How easy is it to get twenty-two men together to play the game of football? In the case of racquetball, however, you can pick up a single person and you're ready for a game.

For a person who wants an effective way to quickly earn aerobic points, playing racquetball is one way to do it. After a forty-five minute session playing racquetball, one comes out feeling much better physically. For those of us who may be up-tight in our work, there is a release from tension after a racquetball game. Many people find that going into a racquetball court and playing the game provides an emotional rejuvination. Enjoyment of the game, and relief from tension may also be accompanied by feeling better mentally after such an activity.

A further benefit from the game is the gregarious nature of the sport. Man is naturally desirous of associating with others of his kind. This is one sport in which good contacts may be established and formed. Benefits may result from both business and social contacts originating in the racquetball court.

In summary I say that playing racquetball can truly add not only days to your life but also life to your days.

When and Where To Play Racquetball

So now to the questions "When and where should we play racquetball?" There are multiple answers. You probably should have started years ago. Like tennis, it's a game to begin playing in your youth because contrary to baseball or football, it's a game you can play throughout your lifetime.

Unlike skiing which can be enjoyed only when or where there is snow, or golf which is played only on green grass, racquetball can be played all year round wherever courts have been constructed. The courts are found at some health clubs, racquet clubs, school or community gymnasiums, military installations (for those in the military services or employed on the bases), YMCA's etc.

So you didn't pick up the game in your youth—no matter. Has your doctor given you the okay? If you have not seen him, it's time you had a physical exam. Having received his clearance, start playing today.

*Grandpa, you've got that game look
on your face!*

How to Play

Racquetball Compared To Tennis and Billiards

In describing racquetball to someone who has never seen the game I would compare it to tennis and billiards.

Racquetball is somewhat like tennis because both games use racquets. The tennis racquet has a longer handle for logical reasons. The tennis court is larger; furthermore, there is rarely a second chance to hit the ball. In racquetball, a missed ball may be pursued and hit on a second attempt off the back wall because (after service has been returned) it is still in play until it has hit the floor twice. The return of a tennis service must get over the net and in bounds, while the return of a racquetball service must get to the front wall before hitting the floor. Also, once the racquetball is in play, there are generally no out-of-bounds so long as the ball reaches the front wall before touching floor. This generally results in more prolonged volleys in racquetball than in tennis, particularly among beginners or average players.

Racquetball is a mixture of tennis and billiards.

In billiards the struck balls take different angled courses on the table depending on the direction of the respective balls at the time they hit the perimeter cushion of the table. The expert billiard player, accordingly, comes to accurately judge the angle that the ball will take after hitting the cushion. In like manner, the racquetball will bounce off the court walls in varying angles depending upon the spin and direction of the ball when it encounters the wall. While there are some similarities between billiards and racquetball incident to judging angles for playing the ball, there is, at the same time, a decided difference applicable to the angles—because a billiard ball rolls on a flat surface and a racquetball bounces inside a cube.

The specific rules for playing racquetball are published by the International Racquetball Association (IRA) and may also be learned by observing and asking about the rules where racquetball is played.

Further, National Racquetball, the magazine published by the United States Racquetball Association has excellent articles on how to play.

Judgment and Reflexes

Reading this book will not make you a good racquetball player. It may, however, help you to enjoy the game if you get into the court and play. As soon as you begin to play, you will observe first hand my comparison of racquetball with tennis and billiards. If you are like the average beginner, the angles of the ball coming off the walls will initially confuse you, and your timing will be off as you attempt to hit the ball. No amount of reading in this book will change that. You have to experience it first hand. So line up a game and begin to play.

After you have played your first game, you will recognize that there are two primary areas of improvement needed to enjoy the game; namely, accurately judging where the ball is going, and developing your reflexes so that your body can physically do what your mind tells it to do with the ball. Once you have come to this conclusion you will find you do not need a companion to play with to develop your judgment and reflexes. This can be done alone in the court.

As a beginner, you may simply want to stand about 10 feet from the front wall. Then patty-cake the ball to the front; and maintain a perpetual volley as the ball rebounds from the front wall. Try returning the ball a dozen times without allowing a second bounce as it comes off the wall. Then try doing it without missing for 50 times. Your reflexes will automatically improve as you are able to return the ball a higher number of times.

Next, lower your aim on the front wall and strike the ball a little harder, returning the ball sometimes with the forehand and sometimes with the backhand. Then hit the ball to the front wall so that it angles back to you off one of the side walls and then off the other side wall. Continue to return the ball, sometimes with the forehand and sometimes with the backhand.

After developing some front court dexterity, try playing a game again. If you were conscientious while practicing alone in the court, you will be pleasantly surprised at the improvement of your reflexes since your first racquetball game.

In subsequent solitary court practice sessions, you would do well to work on the various shots you want to develop which are referred to later in the book.

Let's see ... I hit it like so, and ...

Anticipating the Play

From visual observance, active sports appear to be mostly physical. This is probably true for the young, unthinking, novice. To the experienced athlete, however, there is much that is mental and psychological. As an example I am reminded of a highly publicized prize fight between Duane Bobbick and Ken Norton. Duane Bobbick was the U.S. heavyweight boxer in the 1972 Olympics who turned from amateur to professional; and Ken Norton was the highly respected sparring partner of the heavyweight champion, Mohammed Ali. For half of the first round most of the motions were made by Bobbick as he agressively began the fight. Then there was a right-handed punch thrown from out-of-no-where and the fight was over.

What Bobbick may not have realized, but what was obvious from the outcome, was that Ken Norton gave much mental and psychological thought into a plan for throwing the winning punch. So it should be in racquetball. The mentality that is used before hitting the ball will greatly affect the outcome.

I think of Rick Warner, who was injured in a childhood accident which required the fusion of his right hip. The atrophy of the right leg is noticeably evident by the limp in his walk as he enters the court. You wonder how he will be able to return hard-hit balls during the game. You needn't wonder long, however, when you see Rick in action, for he offers as classic an example of anticipation as I have ever witnessed in the game of racquetball. Rick is a past winner of a Western Regional Masters' Tournament and for years he has appeared in the Seniors' and Masters' finals in Utah racquetball tournaments.

In watching Rick play you detect that there are two minds functioning in his brain —his own and his opponent's. He is obviously mentally reading what his opponent is going to do with the ball, and he is also thinking, "ʼ will keep him guessing at what I'm going to do with this shot." He invariably holds up until the last possible moment before hitting the ball; and then he makes his shot often where the other player least expects it to go, thereby piling up the points against his frustrated antagonist.

By way of reinforcing the importance of anticipation in racquetball, I suggest a careful observation of other players from the gallery. Note the weaknesses prevalent among thoughtless players flailing at the ball as compared with the skillful player who demonstrates in his moves that he is thinking about what his opponent is intending to do with the ball. He then makes it apparent that he has determined where he should be in order to respond to the opposing intention; and he quickly moves to position himself in the correct spot to await the appropriate moment for his handling of the ball.

One person may be slower than another and still play a better game because of superior anticipation. Trey Sayes, Utah's outstanding racquetball player, sums it up this way:

> Anticipation is moving prior to the ball being hit—not afterward. Perfect anticipation is simply being where you need to be. If you don't get there, you can't hit the ball.

Anticipating the Play

Getting Set and Doing Something with the Ball

As you observe from the gallery the racquetball games of novices, you are struck with amazement by the tentative motion and indecisions of the players. Their attempts at properly responsive action are either made prematurely or are too late to effectively hit the ball. Accordingly, you will see all kinds of furious late rushes and various bodily contortions made in desperate lunges to return the ball. Such returns attempted, while wholly off balance, are rarely effective. At best where both sides are playing this type of ball, it will be found that such games will be completely lacking in skill. The sequence ultimately becomes mere batting practice.

To such style of play I've heard Luzell Wilde, a Golden Master player, counsel, "Don't just hit the ball, *do something with it*!" In order to fully understand Lu's admonition, I had to experience having a game with Howard Ringwood who was then Utah State Open Racquetball Champion. After a 21-0 game he counseled me about my weaknesses.

With my feet planted like trunks of oak trees,
I'll kill it this time.

One paraphrased statement still rings clearly in my mind. "You cannot often make an effective shot when you are off balance." The thing to do is to quickly move to where you need to be, and plant your feet into the floor as though they were as firmly rooted as trunks of oak trees. With such balance you can then hit the ball with a precision that often might be comparable to the sure shot of an expert rifleman finding the bull's eye on the target range.

Using Discretion

Having pursuaded you to play racquet-ball, I feel now compelled to say a word about discretion in the game. As observed earlier in the discussion on judgment and reflexes, you should quickly realize that to become skillful in the game you have to know where the ball is going. I offer you now, however, a word of caution.

There is a hazard in looking directly into the backcourt area. This hazard can be overcome in one of two ways: Either use peripheral vision for seeing what is going on in backcourt, or use protective eyeguards. For a $4.50 cash outlay, a pair of eyeguards can be the best insurance you can buy to protect against eye injury in the sport.

As an accountant I depend upon my eyes for a living and they are precious to me. Accordingly, I bought a pair of eyeguards and I wear them constantly when I am playing racquetball. Before buying them, a fast ball struck me just an inch from the eye; and I became aware of others who suffered detatched retinas from balls hit into the eyes.

The best players, of course, are dexterous and can effectively see with the peripheral vision, but I find much comfort in the knowledge that, dexterous or not, I can get into high excitement of the game without being concerned about an errant ball hitting me in the eye.

At times my wife will notice some of the welts on my calves or thighs which were placed there by some opposing player. Upon such occasions she is prompted to remind me, "Just remember that you are a grandpa." or "Are you sure that they are not going to carry you out of the court some day? I want to keep you around, you know." To such comments I have a response, "You don't have to worry, honey, I assure you that I adhere to the motto, 'Discretion is the better part of valor.'"

Accordingly, my pursuit of the ball is predicated upon practical judgment. If there appears to be some doubt about whether I can reach the ball, I'm quick to make the judgment to let it go and conserve my strength for the next volley. It is better to give up the point, than to give up the ghost by way of a coronary.

Center Court Position

In the times that preceded nuclear weaponry, military strategy focused on positions of terrain which could be advantageously used for effective tactical defense, and which could serve as a focal point for mounting a military offense. Such locations would contain significant embattlements to be acquired and defended at great cost. Barricades would be set up, and fortresses erected to secure the advantage of such locations.

In a similar way there is a favored position on the racquetball court. You identify it by an area on the hard wood that is more worn than any other place on the floor. This is because the worn spot has received the central point of action in the court. This is the position for the racquetball player to acquire and hold as much as possible. From this spot you are most often closest to where you need to be to hit the ball, whether to the side, the back, or the front.

Of course, some of your opponent's shots will take you away from center court. On such occasions your being in the center court when your opponent makes his shot, gives you a better opportunity to go where you need to be to return the ball. Upon returning the ball, after having been drawn away from center, you should endeavor to quickly go back to center position before the ball gets to your opponent and he is able to return the ball. If successful, you are again in a strategic spot to meet his best efforts against you. Again quoting Trey Sayes:

> Realistically, anytime that you are between your opponent and the front wall, you have center court position; hence keep his back to the back wall.

*He's controlling center court and
has me running.*

Playing To Win Points

If you follow Lu Wilde's counsel and do something with the ball, your opponent will soon realize that you are in the court not only for exercise but to win points. He soon finds out that your intention to win a point is demonstrated by your attempt to put the ball not only where he "ain't," but to put it where he can't get to it. This will require skill in being able to properly execute a variety of shots.

Now it is time to play solitaire racquetball again. The development of skill comes more from solo practice than it does during the course of the game. During the flurry of the game your reflexes should be doing what comes naturally, and your best shots will be coming from the body physically executing what the mind tells it to do. Just remember:

The more you practice, the better you get. The better you get, the more effective you become.

The Service

The serve is the most important shot (stroke) in the game—Why? It sets the pace (complexion) of subsequent action (rally). DON'T THROW THE SERVE AWAY. Serve with a purpose. There are four advantages to serving:

1. You have center court position.
2. Your opponent's back is to the wall.
3. You are the only person in the world who knows where the ball is going on the serve.
4. You can only score points when you are serving.

Serve generally from the center of the court. From this position you have the best chance to disguise your serve. You don't necessarily serve for aces, but you should strive for a service which will generate a weak return.

The lob serve, the power serve down his weak side, and the cross-court serves (ending up either in the left-hand or right-hand sides of the court) provide a variety of style that will keep your opponent apprehensive about which one will be coming to him next.

The Lob Serve

The lob is not a hard-hit service so it is not speed which mystifies your opponent; rather, pinpoint accuracy is the objective of this serve. It should be hit high on the front wall at an angle so that it barely avoids touching the ceiling and skims the side wall on the opponent's weak side and drops dead in the back corner behind your opponent.

If he tries to take the lob serve in the air before the bounce he scrapes the side wall, thereby losing effectiveness in his return. If he waits for the bounce, he will find the ball in close quarters in the back corner, making it awkward to return the ball. In either event there is often an awkwardness in his return which does not permit him to place the ball in a disadvantageous position for you. Accordingly, the center court position you enjoyed upon serving is still yours; and, with proper anticipation, you can put the ball away where he "aint" and where he cannot reach it.

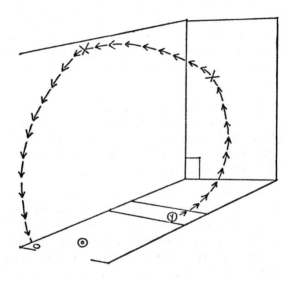

The lob serve.

The Power Serve
To The Weak Side

The power serve requires timing, speed, and accuracy. The change of pace between the lob and power services is significant and may at times bewilder the opponent; he may have come to expect the awkward lob serve. Upon bouncing the ball, preparatory to the power serve, you allow a momentary wait while the ball seems suspended in mid-air; then zip—the quickness of your swing is like the spring of a big cat upon its prey.

An ace power serve will hit the front wall at an angle so that it zooms considerably beyond the short serve line into the crouch where his weak side wall joins the floor, thereby rolling out on the floor.

Ace services are rare, however, and there is a disadvantage which you should recognize in a power service. The hard-hit ball often generates a hard-hit return, and the server (particularly a grandpa lacking sharp dexterity) doesn't have time to set himself up to handle the return. Hence, you may use the power serve as a change of pace, to surprise your opponent. When it works for you, use it; but remember this cardinal rule of serving: "Keep the ball off the back wall" or you may likely lose your serve from a well-executed kill-shot in the return of service.

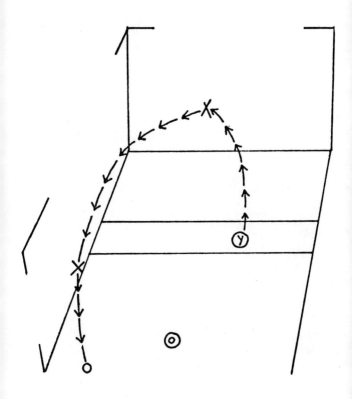

The power serve to the weak side.

The Cross Court Serves

The objectives of these services are to further keep your opponent guessing about what kind of serve he might be getting. The momentary hesitation and swiftness you used for your power serve is also needed in these services so that he fails to anticipate the angles the ball will take.

As server, you must avoid having the ball hit both side walls before touching the floor; otherwise, you have made a fault-service, which takes one of the two chances you are given to make a good service. Depending upon the spin of the ball on the cross-court services, the ball may wind up behind your opponent in the back corner or it may surprisingly come off the side wall at a right angle, thereby catching him by surprise and not allowing him to be ready to strike an effective return of the serve.

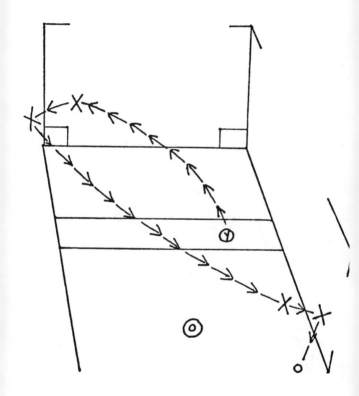

The cross court serve ending in right corner.

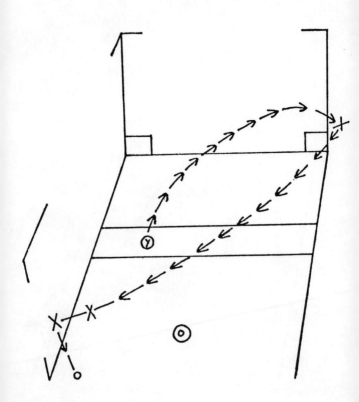

The cross court serve ending in left corner.

Volley

If you are unable to score from your service, a volley may therefore follow which will require some head work as well as dexterity to bring you the points you want.

The Kill Shot

Okay. What shots shall we perfect? I like the kill shot. It strikes low on the front wall an inch or so above the floor. It comes off the front wall as a roll-out on the floor. To me this is the most impressive point play of all racquetball shots. Against such a shot there is no defense and it invariably wins a point for the player who so struck the ball.

How do you perfect such a shot? For me there is a particular place on the front wall upon which I concentrate for desired pinpoint accuracy. If I am playing left side in doubles, it is often the lower left front corner. If I am playing singles or right side in doubles, it's more often the lower right front corner.

Why so? Imagine this reasoning. Whenever my floor position permits; and the location of the opposition favors it, I will attempt to so hit the ball that the following result occurs. The flight of the ball will be low and parallel with the floor. Also, it will be as close and nearly parallel to the side wall as I can make it. Achieving ball flight, which is as close and as nearly parallel to the floor and side wall as possible, is the ultimate shot because the roll-out is a sure point and the ball which sticks to the wall like molasses is the next sure thing.

This I learned from my 21-0 drubbing from Howard Ringwood. Many of my attempted kill shots in that game were not sufficiently close nor parallel to the floor or side walls. Accordingly, from the center court position which he controlled, he could easily get to rebounds from the floor or side walls. On the other hand, I needed a gum scraper to get his shots off the floor or side walls, and all I had was a racquet. So to repeat, low and parallel.

What if you get 50% accuracy? You didn't get the roll-out, but you got a wall clinger. That is still a tough shot to return. If your 50% accuracy is 100% on the low side, you've got a roll-out and a sure point anyhow. Okay. To get the low parallel flight you hit the ball as near to the floor as practicable, surely below the knees and whenever possible at ankle height.

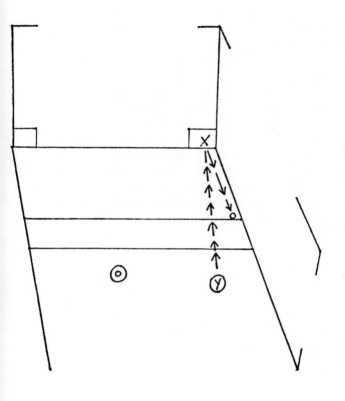

The kill shot to the right front corner.

Only when the element of surprise allows an expert to attempt it, should a low kill shot be attempted above the waist or shoulder height. Such a shot might be effective in tennis but rarely so in the racquetball court. Invariably such a shot either goes into the floor without reaching the front wall, or the opposition takes it on the bounce and wipes you out in the process. Hence, practice diligently hitting into the low corners of the front wall from various positions on the floor. Strips of masking tape one foot long might be used to form a square on the front wall in the corner at the juncture of the floor and the side wall. Concentrated aim for this spot in solitary practice will bring you inner satisfaction when your precision shows up in your later games.

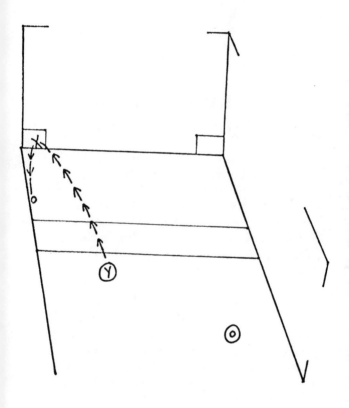

The kill shot to the left front corner.

The Wrap-Around or Soft-Touch Drop Shot

Your position in the court upon hitting the ball may not be in a location which will permit an effective straight kill shot. In this situation, if your opponent is well behind you, the right play may well be a low wraparound drop shot. Depending upon the position of your opponent, the ball should strike low upon either side wall before hitting the front wall. Hopefully, the ball will hit the front wall so low that it will roll out upon the floor. In any event, the ball coming off the front wall should be in a direction away from your opponent. Thus a score may occasionally be made from a soft touch unexpectedly dropped in the front corner which dies before your opponent can reach it. He must, however, be taken completely by surprise by these soft touch or wraparound drop shots, or you will be the amazed one who watches his charge and score upon you.

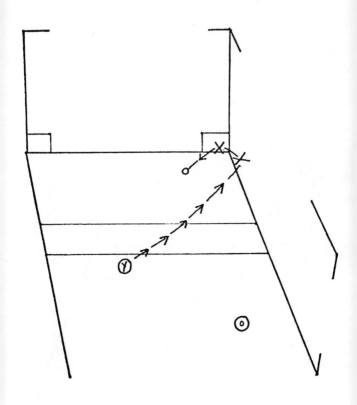

The right wrap around drop shot.

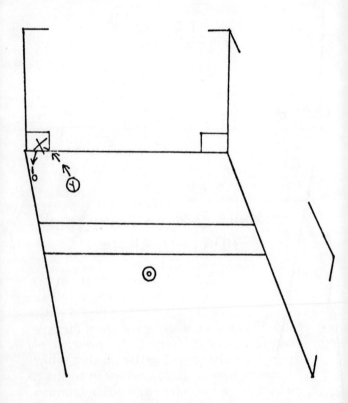

The soft touch drop shot.

Change of Pace From Your Favorite Shots

At times your opponent will be in the favored center court position, while you are in back court. Though you are proud of the relative precision of your kill shot, his presence in center or front court position reduces your chances of getting a shot which he cannot handle. If you persist in trying to make kill shots under such circumstances, your strength often becomes your weakness. Your obsession with your precision, which is at times achieved with your favorite shot, may become your undoing.

Do you think you are the only one who takes notice of your skill with that shot? Indeed not. Your opponent surely remembers the times he was caught in the back court and you whipped in your brand of low shots. He has even taken notice of how you telegraph your intention to make such shots. So what do you think his response is? Why he long ago left his position in back court, and he is now up front having so moved while you were mentally enjoying what you were going to do with your favorite shot. Many is the time I've been scored upon while I was still tingling with pride about the relative precision of my favorite low shot. That was my trouble. My relative precision was not a 100% kill and the anticipation of my opponent was sufficient to scoop up the ball or otherwise smash it to score for him the point I had prematurely thought was mine.

The Passing Shot

Well sir, since you are aware of the fact that your opponent is charging into position to receive your favorite shots, now is the time to smash a passing shot. This is one which travels the court away from where your opponent is heading and one which will drop in the back court while he is on the wrong side or up front where he thought the ball would be.

Timing is the important thing in using the passing shot. The element of surprise makes it effective. How can your opponent concentrate on defending against your kill shots when you distract him and score with surprises? You now have compensated for what was your weakness, an over-reliance on the relative effectiveness of your favorite shot. The important thing is to keep him guessing.

The passing shot is more effective when you delay hitting the ball until the last possible moment. If he is going to successfully defend against your kill shot, he will have to commit himself to the position where he can do so. This is the time you let go with your passing shot.

Some passing shots, however, are ineffective because they remain too long in the air. A high flight and extended rebound off the side or back wall may give your opponent time to change course and handle the rebound. This happens when the passing shot is hit with more zip and abandon than precision. It is therefore important that the passing shot be struck so that the ball will die with a minimum of rebounding. Your opponent will then likely be unable to reach it in time for a good return.

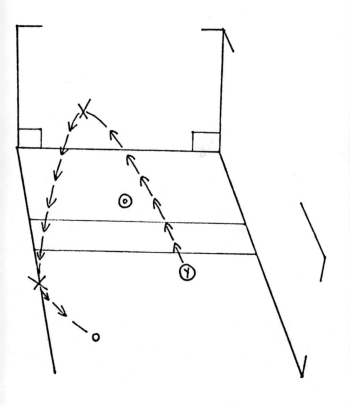

The passing shot.

The Ceiling or High Front Wall Shot

At times your opponent takes you completely out of an offensive position. A good ceiling shot may then be successful in returning him into the back court and enabling you to return and recapture the favored center court position.

Unluckily, your attempted ceiling shot may be inaccurate. The ball may miss the ceiling but hit high on the front wall with such power that it cruises clear to the back wall. Hopefully then, it may rebound from the back wall nearly to the front wall before touching the floor; or it may even strike the front wall again. The successful return of such a ball requires accurate judgment and dexterity. If skillful, however, your opponent may succeed in scoring a soft touch drop shot against you, or in observing your rush to meet such a possibility, he may drive a passing shot which will score upon you.

The ceiling shot is not often used as an offensive one; but is used, hopefully, to gain a position in the court which will be to your advantage. Particularly, the ceiling shot is one that you should use to get your opponent out of his offensive center court position and enable you to return to that favored spot.

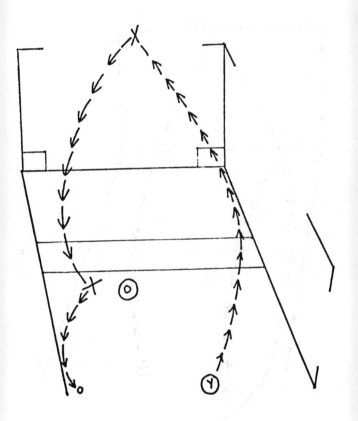

The ceiling shot.

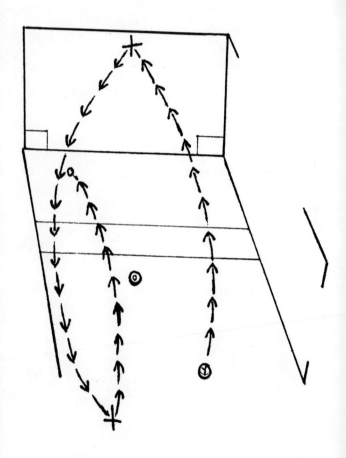

A high front wall shot.

Taboos

Common courtesies in participating sports are found to have their origins in the promotion of goodwill and safety of the participants. Accordingly, fouls are taboo in contact sports to avoid maiming opponents. Teeing-off into golfdom's fairways while players ahead are still within driving range, is also taboo for the same reason.

In like manner, the safety and goodwill of racquetball players will also be considered by those having common courtesy in the racquetball court. Accordingly, if you feel any concern for the health and goodwill of other players, you will avoid the following taboos:

Never open the door of the racquetball court without first looking through the small window in the door to see the conclusion of the volley in process. Then the door should not be opened without first knocking to inform players inside that the door is subsequently being opened. The surprise opening of the door could cause an accident that would seriously injure an unsuspecting player.

Never deliberately obstruct your opponent so that he can not see the ball nor take a clear swing at it. This is an avoidable hinder and is called against the player who so obstructs in tournament play.

Never swing at the ball when to do so may result in hitting a partner or an opponent. If your partner is in the way, you will lose a point by avoiding your swing, but you will perpetuate a friendship. If your opponent is in the way, you should rather call a hinder and have the server begin a replay with a new service of the ball.

"Wanna Play Doubles?"

With the growing popularity of racquetball, I notice an accumulating number of people in the gallery. I see them observing the actions of other players, waiting for their turn in the count-out courts. What an opportunity awaits the mere question, "Want to play doubles?" Not always but often the answer is, "Sure, why not?" Suddenly you are making new acquaintances and taking advantage of the new pattern of play which comes with joining a new set of players.

How's chances of a game? You say you wanna play doubles? Sure, why not?

Admittedly, such an adventuresome approach often brings you into a court with some players who may be carry-overs from the jousting knights of King Arthur's round table. Such a player will be identified by the reckless, wild-swinging manner in which he uses the new weapon which he holds in his hand. With such players it becomes apparent that the once ample 20 x 40 foot playing area has become suddenly crowded.

Some oft-repeated phrases are accordingly appropriate in the initial dialogue among people with whom you have not previously played. "If there is one primary rule in doubles play, it is; 'Call a hinder rather than clobber.' " Where such a rule has not been observed, I have seen some colorful ball brands on the legs, and some gashes across the bridge of the nose from a heavily wielded racquet. As can be seen from the illustration, a handsome profile can suddenly become "Ole waffle face." However, after giving or receiving the primary word of caution and applying such prudence, there is no reason doubles cannot be a safe and enjoyable game.

"Ole waffle face"

"Who's Our Leader?"

Having established the prevailing thought of calling hinders to avoid hazards, the observance of teamwork between the partners will greatly improve the game. This calls for a partnership understanding.

Among "equal" racquetball partners, one will be more "equal" than the other. That is, one partner undoubtedly has a better backhand than the other. Accordingly, if both are righthanders, the one with the better backhand should play the left side. The balls which skim along the left wall will require the best backhand you can manage.

The player taking the left side then should assume the leadership or dominant role. He accordingly should aggressively play the major area of the court, generally considered to be about two-thirds of the floor from front to back as his domain. Hence, he will take balls a little to the right of center because his forehand will generally be better than his partner's backhand.

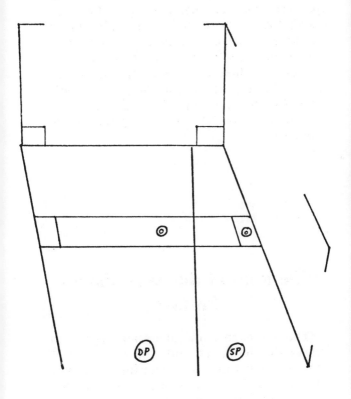

*Sharing the court between dominant
and subordinate partners.*

By the nature of his aggressor role, the so-called "lead" partner may at times be brought out of position, which should be obvious to both partners. For the coming ball, the lead partner may, therefore, say to the other, "Take it!" or the subordinate partner, sizing up the situation, may say, "I've got it!" Whether the judgment is expressed by the dominant partner or by the subordinate partner, the judgment should then be observed, and the action followed through on the basis of such judgment at that time.

The Role of the Subordinate Partner

Having reached an understanding of who plays the dominant and who the subordinate partner roles, the subordinate partner would do well to cast himself in an animated personality and behavior of a mongoose. Years ago in my childhood I saw a movie sequence in which a cobra snake and a mongoose were engaged in mortal combat.

Here's mortal combat.

In the beginning we sensed a frightening feeling for the mongoose who seemed certainly doomed to an untimely death. We simply awaited the instant when the venomous fangs of the cobra would sink into the flesh of the little animal who would then succumb to the tragic bite.

Amazingly, the mongoose avoided the cobra's strike by deftly skirting aside from the powerful lunge of the big snake. As the cobra recoiled, the little animal daringly advanced, all the while keeping an alert watch of the distance between himself and his adversary.

After several futile lunges, wherein the mongoose adroitly avoided contact, the cobra tired. The mongoose then seized upon his solitary opportunity and pounced upon his opponent, sinking his teeth and locking them solidly behind the head of the mighty serpent. Though the cobra writhed mightily, he could not shake loose from the little mongoose, and after some anxious minutes the conflict was over. The cobra lay lifeless upon the ground, a victim of the deceptive, cunning and dexterous mongoose.

In like manner, the subordinate partner in doubles should play the role of the alert mongoose, astutely avoiding the temptation of going after a ball which should rightly be taken by the dominant partner. I've seen many instances in doubles play where an overzealous partner, contrary to the behavior of the mongoose, pursued the ball into his partner's area of the court, only to find he was in the way of an effective return his partner could have made.

Furthermore, I've often seen the subordinate partner, playing the right side, reach over into the center of the court with his backhand to patty-cake a shot to the front wall. Think what would have happened to the mongoose if he had initiated a patty-cake pass at the cobra instead of watching for the correct moment to put him away. In a similar way an inappropriate backhand pat by the subordinate partner allows the opposing team to put the ball away with a smashing kill or passing shot for a sure point completely out of reach.

Hence, a restatement of the principle for the subordinate partner: Hang in there, loose and free, out of the way, allowing the aggressive partner a major share of the court and the action; keeping alert; backing up the dominant partner when needed; and being ready to make the correct shot at the opportune time, often putting the ball away for an impressive point play.

Grandpa's Philosophy About Racquetball

Whether racquetball is a game for you depends upon a number of personal preferences.

Why Racquetball Over Tennis?

Why did this grandpa choose racquetball over tennis? Go back with me to my childhood for the answer to that question.

I lived my early childhood in the small coal mining communities in Carbon County, Utah. These communities were comprised of small clusters of homes located in canyons. Certain communities were divided by forks in the canyons. Part of the homes were built in one fork, while other homes were built in the other fork.

So it was in Spring Canyon where I lived as a boy. Whenever we went to community doings, it meant coming down to the fork in the canyon and backtracking somewhat up the other canyon to the main part of the village.

In typical boy fashion, however, we often would hike up the mountainside from our canyon and drop down the other side of the mountain to the main part of town. We found, moreover, that we were not alone in traversing such terrain for indeed, part of the community had been built upon a flat piece of a mountain ledge where a tennis court was also constructed.

Though I don't remember during those depression years how we came by our tennis racquets, I do recall that we had only one tennis ball. Even though there was a fence around the court, we were continually hitting either "home runs" or "foul balls" which invariably went into the canyon far below. Accordingly, tennis playing usually meant that ninety-nine percent of the time was used in climbing up and down the canyon and searching for our one-and-only-lost-ball while only one percent of the time was spent in playing tennis.

My childhood resolve then was to look for a game in which the ball would be confined to the playing area where ninety-nine percent of the time could be used in playing and only one percent of the time spent in retrieving a ball. Playing racquetball has become the realization of that resolve.

Where's our one and only tennis ball?

Taking Pot-Luck in Getting a Game

In my experience I have found that racquetball can be played with little or no arranging. If playing with someone you know is important to you, you need arrange with only one other person to play singles or with three persons other than yourself to play doubles.

I personally am satisfied to go to the court without prearrangements and take pot-luck in getting into a game. At times I may have wished I had made prior arrangements, but nearly always I am content with the outcome of joining spontaneously into a group which results from the answer to my question, "Would you like to have me join you in a game?"

From such impromptu games I find that I am engaging in a variety of styles. Such variety adapts me to a further development of my own style of play. Furthermore, I find that I am meeting a wider circle of acquantanceships from this gregarious type of activity.

There Are Two Kinds of Racquetball Games

Speaking of the nature of racquetball games, I would classify them into two types: One is for humility and the other is for confidence.

The Game for Humility:

If I had not approached the game of racquetball philosophically, I may have quit playing the game long ago. There is one observation which I have found to be certainly true. The degree of a player's skill is relative. While there are some I can beat 21-0, I have likewise been beaten by that score. Whatever that may indicate, I've not seen a winning player who has not himself been beaten.

Hence comes part of my racquetball philosophy. The games I lose are my games for humility. From such games I take lessons upon which my understanding of the game broadens. How were the points scored against me? What did I do wrong which lost points for me? What did my opponent do right which enabled him to score against me?

My philosophy is that such a game is an impressive way for me to continue learning and improving my game. However, it is also important for my development that I should not be continually found on the short end of lopsided scores. I should be able to take some lessons in humility but it is important to guard against the complete destruction of my ego.

The Game for Confidence:

Equally as important as your games for humility are your games for confidence. I suggest at this point that you arrange to play with your wife or kids or someone who wants to learn about the game. Here is a chance to apply the lessons you learned when you took your beatings. Without the pressure of a killer being in the court you will be surprised at the degree of skill you can develop in applying the shots and the game strategy which were successfully used against you.

Fit Style to Circumstances

How you play the game, in my opinion, should be based upon the circumstances under which you are playing. Under conditions of fairly equal abilities I find enjoyment from the competitive spirit which enters the game.

Tournament Style of Play:

Certainly when engaged in tournament play I sense that my opponent is surely out to beat me; and he surely senses that I mean the same for him. In truth, as a famous chess player stated, "In tournament play, the intention is to destroy the ego of the opponent."

It takes an alert referee in such circumstances to watch the plays closely to assure fairness in the game. He will be expected to call hindrances where there is an obstruction in the way of clearly seeing the ball or returning the shot. The referee becomes indeed an arbitrator between two sides who neither give nor expect quarter from the opposition.

Playing with Novices:

If it is not your intention to play in tournaments, then I feel that your style of play should be very different. Your presence in the court, while serving as a method of exercise, should be to enjoy a sense of comradery in the game. Contrary to the ferocity found in tournaments, the way you play with novices should be based upon their abilities and sensitivity of their feelings.

For example, one pot-luck doubles game brought me into a group consisting of two young men in their late teens and the father of one of the youths. I believe that I shall remain forever ashamed by what occurred while we played.

It was obvious from the beginning that the dad had played a considerable amount of racquetball and that the son had not.

I challenge that call, ref!

After some games in which we switched partners for variety, we ended up pairing the older men against the younger men. From the way the dad was smashing the ball around the court, it was apparent that we should give a handicap to the younger players, so we spotted them 15 points and won.

As though that were not sufficiently satisfying we then spotted them 19 points and first service. They served and then we served without losing a service to win 21-19. It was evident that the dad was intending to show his son how good he was. Such intention was obvious by the way the ball whistled around as though saying, "Here's one down your throat, son."

Though I may never again see the young man and his dad, I shall always wonder about the demoralizing effect such a game must have had upon the son. Indeed, I cannot imagine that from such an experience there would develop a good rapport between the young man and his dad.

Here's one down your throat, son!

Conclusion

Grandpas quite likely have more days of life behind them than ahead of them. They may contradict Robert Browning who said that "the best is yet to be." Such contradiction is accentuated when ill health sets in.

In order to avoid mental depressions and negative attitudes as you grow older, you should do what you can to forestall the deterioration of your health. Prudent physical exercise is the prescription most suitable to conserve well-being, and playing racquetball is an enjoyable way to physically exercise.

You should play the game as vigorously as appropriate to your physical condition and the playing ability of your opponent. Against those of considerable skill, play the best your physical condition will allow. On the other hand, play sportingly with novices.

Play the game as an option for keeping alert and happy so that you "live" your days with a zest for physical activities and associations. Accordingly, get into the court, play racquetball, and enjoy life.

Books About Racquetball

Steve Keeley's "The Complete Book of Racquetball" DBI Books, Inc., Northfield, Illinois

Chuck Leve's "Inside Racquetball," copyrighted by International Racquetball Association $4.95
P.O. Box 12490, Memphis, Tenn. 38112

Jack Fink (2137 Otis Drive, Alameda, Calif. 94501) has written a 20 page manual for beginners entitled "So You're New to Racquetball," $1.50. Other books are also referred to by Jack Fink which include:
"Developing Racquetball Skills" by Vockell and Campbell c/o Dynamic Racquetball Publications Department, P.O. Box 2023, Hammond, Indiana, 46323

"A Game for Everyone" by Randy Stafford 4327 Walnut Grove, Memphis, Tenn. 38117

"Fundamentals of Racquetball" by A. Paul Lawrence

Another racquetball book highly praised by Trey Sayes, who has dominated racquetball in Utah, has been written by Steve Strandemo
4347 Hamilton Street
San Diego, Calif. 92104

RACQUETBALL MEMORABILIA

Notes about experiences, players, appointments, reservations, further tips on how to play, etc.

RACQUETBALL MEMORABILIA

Notes about experiences, players, appointments, reservations, further tips on how to play, etc.

RACQUETBALL MEMORABILIA

Notes about experiences, players, appointments, reservations, further tips on how to play, etc.

RACQUETBALL MEMORABILIA

Notes about experiences, players, appointments, reservations, further tips on how to play, etc.

RACQUETBALL MEMORABILIA

Notes about experiences, players, appointments, reservations, further tips on how to play, etc.

RACQUETBALL MEMORABILIA

*Notes about experiences, players, appoint-
ments, reservations, further tips on how to
play, etc.*

RACQUETBALL MEMORABILIA

Notes about experiences, players, appointments, reservations, further tips on how to play, etc.

RACQUETBALL MEMORABILIA

Notes about experiences, players, appointments, reservations, further tips on how to play, etc.

RACQUETBALL MEMORABILIA

Notes about experiences, players, appointments, reservations, further tips on how to play, etc.

RACQUETBALL MEMORABILIA

Notes about experiences, players, appointments, reservations, further tips on how to play, etc.

RACQUETBALL MEMORABILIA

Notes about experiences, players, appointments, reservations, further tips on how to play, etc.

RACQUETBALL MEMORABILIA

Notes about experiences, players, appointments, reservations, further tips on how to play, etc.

RACQUETBALL MEMORABILIA

Notes about experiences, players, appoint-
ments, reservations, further tips on how to
play, etc.

RACQUETBALL MEMORABILIA

Notes about experiences, players, appointments, reservations, further tips on how to play, etc.

RACQUETBALL MEMORABILIA

Notes about experiences, players, appointments, reservations, further tips on how to play, etc.

RACQUETBALL MEMORABILIA

Notes about experiences, players, appointments, reservations, further tips on how to play, etc.

RACQUETBALL MEMORABILIA

Notes about experiences, players, appointments, reservations, further tips on how to play, etc.

RACQUETBALL MEMORABILIA

Notes about experiences, players, appointments, reservations, further tips on how to play, etc.

RACQUETBALL MEMORABILIA

*Notes about experiences, players, appoint-
ments, reservations, further tips on how to
play, etc.*

RACQUETBALL MEMORABILIA

Notes about experiences, players, appointments, reservations, further tips on how to play, etc.

RACQUETBALL MEMORABILIA

Notes about experiences, players, appointments, reservations, further tips on how to play, etc.

RACQUETBALL MEMORABILIA

Notes about experiences, players, appointments, reservations, further tips on how to play, etc.

RACQUETBALL MEMORABILIA

Notes about experiences, players, appoint-ments, reservations, further tips on how to play, etc.

RACQUETBALL MEMORABILIA

Notes about experiences, players, appointments, reservations, further tips on how to play, etc.

RACQUETBALL MEMORABILIA

Notes about experiences, players, appointments, reservations, further tips on how to play, etc.

RACQUETBALL MEMORABILIA

Notes about experiences, players, appointments, reservations, further tips on how to play, etc.

RACQUETBALL MEMORABILIA

Notes about experiences, players, appointments, reservations, further tips on how to play, etc.

RACQUETBALL MEMORABILIA

Notes about experiences, players, appointments, reservations, further tips on how to play, etc.

RACQUETBALL MEMORABILIA

Notes about experiences, players, appointments, reservations, further tips on how to play, etc.

RACQUETBALL MEMORABILIA

Notes about experiences, players, appointments, reservations, further tips on how to play, etc.

RACQUETBALL MEMORABILIA

Notes about experiences, players, appointments, reservations, further tips on how to play, etc.

RACQUETBALL MEMORABILIA

Notes about experiences, players, appointments, reservations, further tips on how to play, etc.